W9-CFV-216

=GENERALS=
CIVIL of the WAR

=GENERALS= CIVIL WAR

Biographical Sketches of the Principal Leaders

MICHAEL GOLAY

BARNES
&NOBLE
BOOKS
NEW YORK

Produced by DoveTail Books
in association with Saraband Inc.

Copyright © 1997, DoveTail Books
Design copyright © Ziga Design

This edition published by
Barnes & Noble, Inc.
by arrangement with DoveTail Books

1997 Barnes & Noble Books

All rights reserved. No part of this publication may be reproduced,
stored in a retrieval system or transmitted in any form by any means, electronic,
mechanical, photocopying or otherwise, without first obtaining the written
permission of the copyright owner.

ISBN 0-7607-0543-7

Printed in China

9 8 7 6 5 4 3 2 1

All photographs courtesy of the Library of Congress,
Prints and Photographs Division

Contents

Introduction

"Tactics is the art of using troops in battle; strategy is the art of using battles to win the war," according to the nineteenth-century Prussian writer Karl von Clausewitz. At the outset of the Civil War, President Abraham Lincoln faced the challenge of orchestrating an offensive military campaign, because the national forces had to subdue and occupy the rebellious states in order to win and restore the Union. An apparently less complicated task faced the Confederacy: the South could win simply by not losing.

Lincoln himself was inexperienced in military matters, and relied heavily on the advice of his leaders. Commander-in-chief Winfield Scott developed the initial grand strategy, which became known as the "Anaconda Plan": an advance down the Mississippi River to divide the Confederacy and a naval blockade of Southern ports to strangle it.

In July 1861, Union troops under Gen. Irvin McDowell headed for Manassas Junction, Virginia, with the objective of capturing the railroad center. This would allow control of a fast route south to Richmond, the Confederate capital. Union troops attacked early in the morning of July 21. Outnumbered by almost two to one, Confederate troops nevertheless repulsed the attack, thanks in part to the courage of General Thomas Jackson, whose refusal to retreat earned him his famous nickname, "Stonewall." Aided by armies under P.G.T. Beauregard and Joseph E. Johnston, this Southern victory was the first stumbling block for the Union's "grand plan." Confederate leaders followed up with an offensive counterattacking strategy, as Union troops retreated and regrouped.

One year after the First Battle of Manassas, the brilliant Robert E. Lee was placed in command of the Confederacy's main army. Not content to wage defensive warfare, Lee embarked upon a bold invasion of the North, which was first halted on September 17, 1862, at the infamously bloody battle of Antietam. This engagement marked a change in fortunes for the Union's Maj. Gen. George B. McClellan, whose plodding campaign to capture Richmond had been frustrated by Confederate forces led by Lee, Jackson, Johnston, and J.E.B. "Jeb" Stuart, culminating in the Seven Days' Battles of June 1862. The armies of North and South would fight out the eastern-theater war principally on Virginia's soil until July 1863.

The battle of Gettysburg (July 1–3, 1863) is widely considered the turning point in the war in which, thus far, neither side had gained or ceded tangible ground, while the casualties sustained were horrifying—23,000 men had been killed or severely wounded on a single day at Antietam alone. The apparently fearless Jackson had been mortally wounded in Chancellorsville, Virginia, in May 1863. In effect, the Confederates had maintained the strategic upper hand, in that they had blocked the Union advance. This had been accomplished with less economic power and significantly inferior troop numbers under remarkable tactical leadership, whose decisive direction had capitalized on every opportunity to surprise the advancing Northerners and to counterattack aggressively. However, at Gettysburg, in Lee's second major invasion of the North, Confederate troops were repulsed, and their numbers and resources were at last so weakened as to make their costly counteroffensive strategy seem barely viable. Lee's troops managed to escape and retreat, but the Union was no longer under such relentless pressure.

In May 1864, Ulysses S. Grant, recently appointed overall commander of Union forces, initiated a second campaign for Richmond, where Confederate troops were now securely entrenched. At the battle of Cold Harbor, June 1–3, 1864, Lee's heavily fortified troops held off the attackers. Having sustained a disastrous 12,000 casualties at Cold Harbor, Grant targeted the Confederate supply line: the railroad and communications center of nearby Petersburg, Viriginia. Thus began a nine-month siege of Richmond.

By this time, the naval blockade of Confederate ports, which had been largely ineffective during the early part of the war, had tightened. The 600 or so Federal warships on patrol by 1864 reduced the blockade runners' chances of successful supply runs—with much-needed arms—from nine in ten (as in 1861) to a mere one in three. The ports were sealed off, and the Anaconda Plan was taking effect.

From an initially conventional war that had resembled established tactical models, the Civil War had slowly evolved into what is now regarded as the first modern conflict. Railroads and the telegraph provided communications with much greater range, while cannon and the increasing use of defensive field fortifications saw the emergence of trench warfare, which would become the model for World War I. Lee in particular used these innovations and modern strategic devices brilliantly, but Grant's concentration on the economic war would prove even more compelling. As Richmond's population starved and supplies to factories were cut off, the war of attrition sapped Confederate morale as much as its more readily quantifiable resources. Troops deserted, and civilians rioted for bread. On April 2, 1865, Lee ordered the evacuation of Richmond and, one week later, surrendered to Grant at Appomattox Court House, Virginia.

While the most ostensibly crucial events of the war were played out in and around Virginia, generals fought noteworthy strategic campaigns elsewhere. Jefferson Davis entrusted the defense of the South's heartland to Albert Sidney Johnston, whose war record was, in fact, characterized by almost unremitting defeat. Braxton Bragg fared better in a valiant defense of Tennessee, keeping open important industrial centers and agricultural territory for the Confederacy until late 1863. William T. Sherman, considered by some the Union's best strategist and most able general, led his forces in an extraordinary thousand-mile series of campaigns (1864–5) from Tennessee through Georgia, and on to southern Virginia. In all arenas, many men distinguished themselves as great military leaders.

The Civil War would profoundly affect not only the future of the United States, which would thenceforward recognize all her citizens as "forever free," but the strategy and tactics of major-scale warfare around the world until well into the twentieth century. Quick to adapt to technological change, and shifting fortunes by economic as well as military strategy, these great generals put an end to outmoded thinking and earned, fully deserving, their lasting place in world history.

Chronology

1859

Oct. 16–18 John Brown's raid on Harpers Ferry.

1860

Nov. 6 Abraham Lincoln elected president of the United States.

Dec. 20 The first Southern state, South Carolina, secedes.

1861

Jan. Five more states secede: Mississippi (1/9); Florida (1/10); Alabama (1/11); Georgia (1/19); Louisiana (1/26).

Feb. 1 Texas secedes.

Feb. 18 Jefferson Davis inaugurated president of the Confederacy.

Mar. 4 Inauguration of President Abraham Lincoln.

Apr. 12–13 Fort Sumter is captured by CSA troops.

Apr. 15 Lincoln calls for 75,000 volunteers to put down the rebellion.

Apr. 17 Virginia secedes.

Apr. 18 USA troops abandon the Federal armory at Harpers Ferry, Va.

Apr. 20 Colonel Robert E. Lee resigns from the U.S. Army.

May 6 The Confederacy recognizes a state of war. Arkansas secedes.

May 20 North Carolina secedes. Kentucky's governor issues a proclamation of neutrality.

June 8 Tennessee secedes, the last state to join the Confederacy.

July 21 The First Battle of Manassas (Bull Run), a CSA victory.

Aug. 10 The battle of Wilson's Creek, Missouri, a CSA victory.

1862

Feb. 13–16 Fort Donelson, Tennessee, falls to the USA.

Feb. 25 USA forces capture Nashville, Tennessee.

Mar. 6–8 Battle of Pea Ridge, Arkansas, a USA victory.

Mar. 8–9 The ironclad C.S.S. *Virginia* (known as the *Merrimack)* defeats frigates U.S.S. *Cumberland* and *Congress,* and engages the ironclad U.S.S. *Monitor;* battle ends in a draw.

Mar. 17 McClellan begins the Peninsula Campaign for Richmond.

Mar. 23 Lincoln orders Gen. McDowell's troops to defend Washington, D.C., in case it is threatened by Jackson.

Apr. 6–7 USA forces attacked at Shiloh, Tenn., but hold it. CSA commander Gen. Albert Sidney Johnston is killed.

Apr. 11 Fort Pulaski, Georgia, surrenders to the USA.

Apr. 25 The Federal fleet captures New Orleans.

May 3 Confederates evacuate Yorktown, Va.

June 1 General Lee is given command of the Army of Northern Virginia.

June 6 USA troops capture Memphis, Tenn.

June 9 The Shenandoah Valley Campaign ends with CSA victory.

June 25 The Seven Days' campaign begins with the battle of Oak Grove, Va.

July 2 Seven Days' Campaign ends as USA troops retreat.

July 17 Grant is given command of the USA armies in the West.

Aug. 27–28 CSA forces begin campaign into Tennessee and Kentucky.

Aug. 29–30 The Second Battle of Manassas (Bull Run), a CSA victory.

Sep. 4 Lee begins the Confederates' first invasion of the North.

Sep. 15 CSA troops capture Harpers Ferry, Va.

Sep. 17 Battle of Antietam (Sharpsburg), a USA victory.

Oct. 9–12 Jeb Stuart's raid in the North takes him as far as Chambersburg, Penn.

Dec. 11–14 USA forces attack Fredericksburg, Virginia, a CSA victory.

1863

Jan. 1 The Emancipation Proclamation, first announced by Abraham Lincoln after Antietam, takes effect.

Mar. 3 USA Conscription Act, calling for the enlistment of all able-bodied male citizens aged 20 to 45, is passed.

Apr. 2 Richmond is wracked by the bread riot.

Chronology

May 1–4 The Battle of Chancellorsville, Va., a CSA victory. Gen. Jackson mortally wounded by his own men.

May 19–22 USA siege of Vicksburg, Miss., begins.

June 3 Lee begins his second invasion of the North.

June 20 West Virginia officially becomes the 35th state of the USA.

July 1–3 The Battle of Gettysburg, a USA victory, and a turning point in the war.

July 4 After a six-week siege, Vicksburg falls to the USA. Lee retreats from Gettysburg.

July 13–16 Draft riots in New York and other Northern cities; nearly 1,000 killed or wounded.

Aug. 8 Lee offers to resign the command of the Army of Northern Virginia, pleading ill health. President Davis refuses.

Sep. 2 USA troops occupy Knoxville, Tenn., cutting the railroad link to Virginia.

Sep. 19–20 Battle of Chickamauga, Tenn., a CSA victory.

Nov. 19 Lincoln delivers the Gettysburg Address.

Nov. 23–25 Battle of Chattanooga (Missionary Ridge), USA victory.

1864

Jan. 19 The Arkansas pro-union Constitutional Convention adopts an antislavery constitution.

Mar. 10 Grant is put in command of the Armies of the United States.

May 4 Grant begins the Wilderness Campaign.

May 5–6 Battle of the Wilderness, inconclusive.

May 7–29 Sherman moves toward Atlanta.

June 1–3 The Battle of Cold Harbor, CSA victory.

June 8 Lincoln is nominated for a second term.

June 16–18 Siege of Petersburg begins.

June 27 Battle of Kennesaw Mountain, CSA victory.

July 27–29 The siege of Atlanta.

Sep. 1 CSA Gen. Hood evacuates Atlanta.

Oct. 22 Hood begins the Tennessee campaign.

Nov. 8 Lincoln is re-elected, with Andrew Johnson as vice president.

Nov. 16 Sherman leaves Atlanta for the "March to the Sea."

Nov. 25 CSA attempt to burn New York City fails.

Dec. 15–16 Battle of Nashville, USA victory.

1865

Jan. 31 The CSA Congress names Robert E. Lee General-in-Chief of all the Southern armies. United States House passes the Thirteenth Amendment.

Feb. 1 Sherman begins march through the Carolinas.

Feb. 17 Confederates evacuate Charleston.

Mar. 4 Lincoln is inaugurated for a second term.

Mar. 11 Sherman takes Fayetteville, North Carolina.

Mar. 13 The Confederate Congress authorizes the recruitment of black soldiers.

Apr. 2 The assault on Petersburg begins. CSA evacuates Richmond.

Apr. 3 Richmond occupied by Federal troops.

Apr. 9 Lee surrenders to Grant at Appomattox Court House. The stage is set for the general surrender of Southern forces.

Apr. 14 Lincoln is shot by John Wilkes Booth at Ford's Theatre in Washington, D.C.

Apr. 17 Johnston asks Sherman for terms of surrender.

May 10 Davis is captured near Irwinville, Ga. President Johnson proclaims the end of armed resistance.

May 12 Battle of Palmito Ranch, Tex., the last land fight of the war.

June 23 President Johnson declares Federal blockade of Southern states at an end.

July 7 Lincoln assassination conspirators executed.

Dec. 18 Thirteenth Amendment to the Constitution is declared "in effect."

THE

UNION

Abraham Lincoln,
President of the United States

NATHANIEL P. BANKS

1816–94
Birthplace:
Waltham, Massachusetts
Senior Command:
Department of the Gulf,
1863–64

A career politician, a veteran member of Congress, and an antebellum governor of Massachusetts, Nathaniel Banks used his political contacts to obtain a major general's commission in May 1861, relieving General Robert Patterson of his command. In the event, Banks proved far more successful at winning elections than at winning battles.

General Banks became Stonewall Jackson's foil in Jackson's brilliant Shenandoah Valley campaign of 1862. Later that year, he was transferred west to command the Department of the Gulf, replacing B.F. Butler. Though messy, his Red River Campaign of 1863 earned him the Thanks of Congress and yielded the fall of Port Hudson on the Mississippi, but only after the capture of Vicksburg had made the downriver fortress untenable.

Banks's failed Red River Campaign of 1864 led to his resignation from field command. He returned to political life after the war, serving several more terms in Congress (1865–78; 1888–91).

Samuel R. Curtis

1805–66
Birthplace:
Champlain, New York
Senior Command:
Army of the Southwest;
Department of Kansas, 1862

An 1831 West Point graduate, Samuel Curtis left the army after a year and eventually entered the law and politics. At the outbreak of the Civil War, he resigned his Iowa congressional seat (1856–61) to become colonel of the 2nd Iowa Volunteer Infantry.

Rising rapidly to commander of the Army of the Southwest, he defeated a Confederate army led by Major General Earl Van Dorn at the battle of Pea Ridge, Arkansas, in March 1862. After a difficult 1,000-mile march in July and August, Curtis captured Helena, Arkansas, securing yet another victory for the Union. In September he was appointed commander of the Department of the Missouri. Curtis also served as commander of the Departments of Kansas and the Northwest.

In 1864 troops under Curtis's command checked Sterling Price's Missouri Raid of 1864, a battle that cost Price thousands of small arms, all his cannon, and most of his men. After the war, Curtis was appointed an Indian commissioner.

George Armstrong Custer

1839–76
Birthplace:
New Rumley, Ohio
Senior Command:
Cavalry Div., Army of
the Shenandoah, 1864–65

Newly graduated from West Point, Custer joined the Army of the Potomac in 1861 and commanded a cavalry brigade with distinction at First Bull Run (Manassas). His reputation as a fearless leader grew as he fought throughout the Peninsular Campaign of 1861–62. At the age of twenty-three, he became the youngest general in the Union Army.

Many of those who served under Custer (called "the boy general") admired him; others accused him of recklessness and glory hunting. He would remain a controversial figure throughout his career, but his Civil War record was outstanding. In 1863 he pursued Confederate forces retreating from Gettysburg and engaged them at Battle Mountain, Virginia. His greatest triumph came in 1865, when he hounded Lee's retreating army until the surrender at Appomattox. It was Custer who accepted the Confederate flag of truce. After the war, he joined the Seventh Cavalry Regiment and fought in the Sioux Wars until the fated ambush of 1876 at the Little Big Horn River.

ULYSSES S. GRANT

1822–85
Birthplace:
Point Pleasant, Ohio
Senior Command:
General in Chief
of the Union Army, 1864–65

A tanner's son, Hiram Ulysses Grant grew up in strait-ened circumstances, though, unlike many western-ers of his time, he managed to attend school more or less regularly up until age seventeen. He was an indifferent student but a gifted handler of horses, and he never lost his boyhood fellow-feeling for animals. Later in life he disapproved of killing them, even for food, espe-cially, as he put it, "if they went on two legs."

Listed wrongly as "Ulysses S. Grant" when he arrived at West Point in 1839, he dropped Hiram and adopted his mother's maiden name, Simpson, as his second name, spar-ing the army the pain of admitting a mistake. His acad-emy career was otherwise undistinguished. He graduated 21st in his class of 39 in 1843.

As a young infantry officer, Grant served in Missouri and Louisiana and fought in the Mexican War. In 1848 he married Julia Dent and looked ahead to a life of routine in the regular army. But Grant failed miserably as a peace-time soldier. Bored, lonely, and increasingly addicted to drink, he resigned under pressure in 1854. Grant fared little better in civil life. He moved from job to job, at one point selling firewood in the streets of St. Louis. In 1860, with nowhere else to turn, he went to work as a clerk in his brother's dry goods store in Galena, Illinois.

Those were bitter years, as Grant acknowledged later — toward the end of the Civil War, when a number of wealthy New Yorkers presented him with a handsome military overcoat at a ceremonial occasion. He had become a national idol, his future assured. He tried on the coat, and after a few moments' silence, reflected somberly: "There have been times in my life when the gift of an overcoat would have been an act of charity. No one gave it to me when I needed it. Now when I am able to pay for all I need, such gifts are continually thrust upon me."

The coming of the war had reversed Grant's fortunes almost overnight. In September 1861, he was appointed brigadier general of the Cairo (Ill.) military district. "Be careful," his father warned him. "You're a general now; it's a good job, don't lose it." Within eighteen months, Grant had made his military reputation. A bold strategist and a master of logistics, his list of successes mounted: capture of Forts Henry and Donelson in February 1862; recovery from near-disaster and eventual victory at Shiloh in April of that year; the brilliant overland campaign in the spring of 1863 that yielded one of the war's decisive victories — the surrender of the Confederate fortress of

Vicksburg. His victory at Missionary Ridge near Chattanooga in November 1863 opened the invasion route to Atlanta and the Deep South and led to Grant's ascension to commander-in-chief of all Union land forces.

Coming east in the winter of 1864, he made his headquarters in the field with the Army of the Potomac. On May 4, 1864, he opened a relentless campaign against Robert E. Lee's Army of Northern Virginia. In a continuous shifting battle from the Wilderness to Cold Harbor, he ground down Lee's army mercilessly. "I propose," he wired in a famous dispatch after the drawn battle of Spotsylvania Court House, "to fight it out on this line if it takes all summer."

Casualties mounted to unprecedented levels, but he pressed on all the same. "I can't spare this man," Lincoln had said after Shiloh, when Grant's critics sought his removal from command. "He fights." But Grant was no mere slugger. He was a thinking soldier of rare ability. In June 1864, after a surprise crossing of the James River, he forced Lee into defensive lines around Petersburg and Richmond, robbing the Confederates of all freedom of movement. Lee never again resumed the offensive. Some analysts have called the James crossing the most brilliant Union operation of the entire war.

The 1864 battles cost the Army of the Potomac 66,000 casualties between May 4 and June 19—half the army's strength at the outset of the campaign—but Grant refused to turn away from his goal. With simplicity and directness of purpose, he pursued his strategy to the end: destruction of the Confederate armies, one by one.

Grant's last campaign opened on March 29, 1865, with a wide swing around the Confederate right beyond Petersburg. Cavalry and infantry under Gen. Philip Sheridan turned Lee's flank at Five Forks on April 1. "If the thing is pressed, I think Lee will surrender," Sheridan wrote Grant on April 6 as Lee limped westward. Grant passed the message on to President Lincoln. "Let the thing be pressed," the president replied.

The Army of Northern Virginia surrendered to Grant at Appomattox Court House on April 9. That night jubilant Union forces fired off cannon salutes and exploded now-surplus small arms ammunition in a grand fireworks display. Grant brusquely ordered a halt to the celebrations. "The war is over," he said. "The rebels are our countrymen again." The other Confederate armies soon followed Lee's example. Grant accepted the Republican nomination for president in 1868 and his party won a landslide victory in November. He was re-elected in 1872.

Grant's two presidential terms were marred by scandal and corruption on a grand scale. No one ever suggested Grant himself had stolen while in office; in fact, he left the White House with a modest net worth of only a few thousand dollars. But he knew one final triumph — the completion, just before his death on July 23, 1885, of his *Personal Memoirs*, a best-seller in its time and an enduring classic of Civil War literature.

JOSEPH HOOKER

1814—79
Birthplace:
Hadley, Massachusetts
Senior Command:
Army of the Potomac, 1863

Vain, self-applauding "Fighting Joe" Hooker, whose grandfather was a Revolutionary War officer, graduated from West Point in 1837 and fought in Mexico before resigning from the army in 1853 to take up farming in Sonoma, California.

He accepted a Union commission at the start of the war and led a division on the Peninsula and a corps at Antietam. After Fredericksburg, he succeeded Burnside, against whom he had schemed, in command of the Army of the Potomac. In May 1863, he launched a campaign that he boasted would destroy the Army of Northern Virginia. Instead, Hooker became the victim of the most brilliant of Lee's victories, Chancellorsville.

Removed from command on the eve of Gettysburg and transferred west, he led two corps under Grant at Chattanooga. Passed over for command of one of Sherman's armies in 1864, he asked to be relieved of duty and never returned to the field, though he remained in the service until he suffered a stroke in 1868.

GEORGE B. McCLELLAN

1826–85
Birthplace:
Philadelphia, Pennsylvania
Senior Command:
General in Chief
of the Union Army, 1861–62

Apparently a favorite of fortune, George B. McClellan was born into a prominent Philadelphia family, graduated second in his West Point class of 1846, successfully served in the Mexican War, and became president of a railroad at the age of thirty-one.

McClellan succeeded to the command of the Union Army of the Potomac after the disaster at Bull Run (Manassas) in July 1861. A brilliant organizer, he inspired devotion in his troops and transformed the army. In the field, though, he lacked dash and aggressiveness.

His caution was legendary. "If McClellan is not using the army," President Lincoln once said, "I should like to borrow it for a while." He advanced so slowly toward Richmond in the spring of 1862 that his critics dubbed him the "Virginia Creeper." At Antietam, he missed several opportunities to crush the Confederate army.

Lincoln relieved McClellan after Antietam and he never saw field service again. In 1864 he was once again defeated by Lincoln, this time for the presidency.

George G. Meade

1815–72
Birthplace:
Cadiz, Spain
Senior Command:
Army of the Potomac,
1863–65

The Union victor at Gettysburg, George Meade rates as a solid, if unspectacular, commander, cautious and careful in the field despite his ungovernable temper. Born in Cadiz, Spain, Meade grew up in Pennsylvania and graduated from West Point in 1835.

In 1862 and 1863, he performed capably as a division and corps commander at Antietam, Fredericksburg, and Chancellorsville. In June 1863, Meade was chosen by Lincoln to replace Hooker as commander of the Army of the Potomac, a position he quickly accepted. Praised for his efficient handling of troops at Gettysburg, he has been faulted for failing to pursue the wounded and vulnerable Army of Northern Virginia after the battle.

Meade remained in nominal command of the Army of the Potomac after Grant came east in 1864. However, he played a secondary role to that of Grant's protégé Sheridan in the pursuit to Appomattox in April 1865, the campaign that brought the long war to an end. In 1872 Meade succumbed to a wound that he had received a decade earlier.

John Pope

1822–92
Birthplace:
Louisville, Kentucky
Senior Command:
Department of Northwest,
1862 and 1863–65

An 1842 West Point graduate and an Old Army veteran, John Pope rose swiftly to senior command in the West. By late 1862, his success in clearing New Madrid and Island No. 10 of Confederates had opened the Mississippi River almost as far as Memphis.

Lincoln chose him in the summer of 1862 to replace the popular McClellan as commander of the Army of the Potomac. With a bombastic opening address in which he questioned the courage of his troops, Pope alienated himself from them at the outset, and things quickly got worse. Robert E. Lee humbled him at the second battle of Bull Run on August 29–30, 1862, thoroughly outwitting him and inflicting heavy casualties on his army. Despite Pope's claims that his subordinates were to blame, Lincoln relieved him of command the next day.

Although Pope was never chosen to be a field commander after the Bull Run disaster, he held a series of district and department commands during the 1860s and '70s. He officially retired from the service in 1886.

WILLIAM S. ROSECRANS

1819–98
Birthplace:
Kingston, Ohio
Senior Command:
Army of the Cumberland,
1862–63

Ohio-born William S. Rosecrans, an 1842 West Pointer, interrupted a successful career as an engineer to return to the army at the start of the Civil War, where he joined McClellan as a volunteer aide-de-camp.

In spite of a notoriously unruly temper, Rosecrans was chosen to replace John Pope as commander of the Mississippi Army in June 1862. He was quickly promoted to major general and led the Union Army of the Cumberland to a disputed victory (the Confederates claimed a draw) at Stone's River near Murfreesboro, Tennessee, in late 1862. His solid performance at Stone's River earned him the Thanks of Congress.

Rosecrans's embarrassing defeat at Chickamauga in September 1863 resulted in his removal from command. Although he was commander of the Missouri Department until 1864, he saw no further service in the field. He enjoyed postwar success in business and in public service, representing California in Congress (1881–85) and serving as a register of the U.S. Treasury (1885–93).

Philip H. Sheridan

1831–88
Birthplace:
Albany, New York
Senior Command:
Army of the Shenandoah,
1864–65

The son of Irish immigrants, future commander Philip H. Sheridan was raised in frontier Ohio, where his father had migrated in search of work on the canals and railroads. He was educated in the village school of Somerset, Ohio, and worked as a store clerk there before accepting a West Point cadetship in 1848. The fiery, volatile Sheridan soon landed in difficulties at the military academy. Suspended for a year for threatening an older cadet with a bayonet, he returned, managing to stay just on the right side of academy law to graduate an undistinguished 34th of 49 in the Class of 1853.

He served in Texas and fought Native Americans in the Pacific Northwest during the later 1850s, but nothing in his prewar army career suggested he would become one of the great American field commanders. The outbreak of the Civil War found him in Missouri as quartermaster and commissary for Gen. Samuel Curtis's Army of the Southwest. A sloppy bookkeeper, careless of the rules, he did not survive in the job long and barely escaped a court martial. He joined Henry Halleck's staff as a doer of odd jobs, at one point taking on a roving assignment buying remounts for the Missouri command.

In May 1862, Sheridan wangled a commission as colonel of the 2nd Michigan Cavalry. Within two months, he had risen to command of a brigade. He seemed born for the wild excitement of battle. His aggressive handling of cavalry won him promotion and an infantry command. In October he led a division at the battle of Perrysville, Kentucky. His stubborn refusal to give ground at Stone's River, Tennessee, in December helped save Gen. William Rosecrans's army from defeat. Not long after Stone's River, Sheridan won promotion to major general. He saw action at Chickamauga in September 1863. In November, under Ulysses S. Grant, he led the impulsive charge up Missionary Ridge near Chattanooga that ended in a complete Confederate rout.

Sheridan came east with Grant in March 1864, to take charge of the 10,000-man Cavalry Corps of the Army of the Potomac. His first independent cavalry operation, the Richmond Raid of May 9–24, 1864, proved an unqualified success. On May 11, his troopers defeated the Confederate cavalry of J.E.B. Stuart at Yellow Tavern; Stuart was mortally wounded in the battle. Sheridan went on to ride completely around Lee's army, wrecking railroad track, destroying supplies, and spreading alarm in the Southern capital.

Sheridan's greatest success came in the Shenandoah Valley in the late summer and autumn of 1864. Grant ordered him to destroy a small Confederate army under Jubal Early, then devastate the Shenandoah, the eastern Confederacy's granary, "so that crows flying over it will have to carry their provender with them." Sheridan defeated Early at Winchester on September 19 and at Fisher's Hill on September 22, but Early regrouped. On October 19, the Confederates surprised Sheridan's command at Cedar Hill, while Sheridan himself was away in Washington. Making his famous ride from Winchester, Sheridan reached the battlefield just in time to rally his forces and turn an embarrassing defeat into a smashing victory. He then turned to the business of destruction. "The people must be left with nothing but their eyes to weep with over the war," he told his officers. In a post-campaign report to Grant, he claimed to have burned 2,000 barns and 700 mills.

Grant gave Sheridan a starring role in the last campaign of March–April 1865. His rout of the Confederates at Five Forks on April 1, 1865, flanked Lee out of the Petersburg defenses and forced him into a ragged westward retreat. Sheridan, with cavalry and infantry, pursued without letup. He smashed part of Lee's army at Sayler's Creek on April 6, and trapped the remnants at Appomattox Court House on April 9. Lee surrendered to Grant that afternoon. Sheridan is said to have made off with the most sought-after souvenir of that historic day: the desk where Lee signed the fateful document by which the Army of Northern Virginia passed into history.

Philip H. Sheridan

Barely five feet tall, squat and solidly built, with close-cropped hair that had the look of being painted onto his scalp, Sheridan possessed a fighter's instincts and a natural air of authority on the battlefield. His soldiers called him "Little Phil" and responded enthusiastically to his pugnacious example. "Smash 'em up, smash 'em up!" he used to call out madly in the midst of a battle. The journalist Sylvanus Cadwallader, who knew Grant well, always claimed the commanding general held Sheridan above all others, even Sherman, in esteem.

In May 1865, Sheridan took charge of a 50,000-strong U.S. army on the Rio Grande in Texas, a show of force meant to overawe the French in Mexico. He later served as postwar governor of Texas and Louisiana, where he enforced Reconstruction policies so aggressively that President Johnson arranged his recall.

As a senior commander in the postwar army, Sheridan organized a series of punitive expeditions against the Plains Natives in the 1870s. The infamous dictum that "The only good Indian is a dead Indian" is one version of a phrase allegedly used by Sheridan in 1870: "The only good Indians I ever saw were dead." He led the Marias River massacre in Montana, in which 173 Piegans were brutally slaughtered, a third of them women and children.

In 1884 Sheridan became second in succession to Grant as army commander-in-chief. His *Personal Memoirs* were published in 1888, only a few days before he died in Nonquitt (near Bedford), Massachusetts.

William T. Sherman

1820–91
Birthplace:
Lancaster, Ohio
Senior Command:
Western Department, 1864

Sherman's admirers rate him perhaps the outstanding Federal commander of the Civil War. His masterly marches of 1864–65 carried Union forces a thousand miles, from Chattanooga through Georgia and the Carolinas to the southern reaches of Lee's Virginia — campaigns of maneuver that doomed the main Confederate army around Richmond and hastened the collapse of the rebellion.

The son of a jurist, prominent in his home state, he was orphaned at the age of nine and raised by a well-to-do friend of his parents', Thomas Ewing. He received his early education at a local academy, entered West Point in 1836, and graduated four years later, a solid sixth in his class.

Entering the army as an artillery second lieutenant, Sherman saw service in Florida and in California during the Mexican War. Garrison and survey duty in South Carolina and Georgia provided unwitting preparation for his later career, when his troops would credit him with a virtually encyclopedic knowledge of every road, path and byway in the two rebel states.

For the most part, though, Sherman found peacetime army life dull and unchallenging. Bored and frustrated by the slow pace of promotion, he resigned in 1853 to become a banker. Like many soldiers of his era, he knew little success in civil life. He failed at banking, then turned to the law. He lost his only case.

Sherman returned to the cloistered life in 1859 as superintendent of the Louisiana Military Academy. From this vantage, he witnessed the rise of the secession movement from up close, and agonized over the breakup of the Union. When it came finally, he turned down the offer of a Confederate commission and in May 1861 accepted the colonelcy of the 13th U.S. Infantry, a regular unit.

Sherman commanded a division under Grant at Shiloh in 1862, the beginning of the most successful Union military partnership of the war. Grant thereafter gave him leading roles in the decisive Vicksburg and Chattanooga campaigns of 1863. In March 1864, he succeeded Grant as the senior Federal commander in the West.

In a much-quoted passage, the young Massachusetts officer John Gray described the red-haired, red-bearded Ohioan as "the concentrated essence of Yankeedom, tall, spare and sinewy, a very homely man, with a regular nest of wrinkles in his face." He was nervous, voluble, and conversant on an astonishing range of subjects. His soldiers idolized him for his competence, his care with their lives, and his disdain for the romantic view of war. "Its glories are all moonshine," he once said of battle, "even success the most brilliant is over dead and mangled bodies, with the anguish and lamentation of distant families."

In May 1864, Sherman launched the grand offensive that, in combination with Grant's vise-grip on Lee in Virginia, closed out the war in less than a year. After a four-month campaign of maneuver, his army drove the Confederates out of Atlanta, next to Richmond the South's most important military target. "Atlanta is ours and fairly won," he wired Washington exultantly.

Almost at once, Sherman began preparations for his famous March to the Sea. Grant was skeptical at first. "I can make this march," Sherman insisted. "I can make Georgia howl. If you can whip Lee and I can march to the Atlantic, I think Uncle Abe will give us 20 days' leave of absence to see the young folks." "Go on, then, as you propose," Grant wired.

Setting out on November 15, 1864, the 60,000-strong army blazed a 60-mile-wide trail of destruction through the heart of Georgia. The two-month campaign showed Southerners that the Confederacy could no longer protect them: it cut the deep south off from Virginia, and it denied food, forage and military necessities to Lee's hungry army in Virginia. Sherman ordered his troops to leave nothing of value — from crops to railways — in their wake. In December, after a remarkable 325-mile march from Atlanta to the sea, Sherman offered President Lincoln a Christmas gift of Georgia's city of Savannah, "with 150 heavy guns and plenty of ammunition, also about 25,000 bales of cotton."

After resting the army for six weeks, Sherman opened the Campaign of the Carolinas—a longer, more difficult and more decisive operation, Sherman always believed, than the Georgia march. Union forces wreaked a terrible vengeance on South Carolina. Careless and arsonous troops, Rebel and Yankee, burned out the heart of Columbia, the state capital. Charleston, the cradle of secession, fell with hardly a shot fired. Battles at Averasboro and Bentonville in North Carolina barely slowed Sherman's advance. On April 26, 1865, he accepted the surrender of Confederate forces in the Carolinas, effectively ending the Civil War in the East.

Sherman's campaigns were noteworthy for their promiscuous destruction of property and their comparatively low casualty rates. He preferred maneuver to frontal assault and held that the war would end only when its realities were brought home starkly to the civilian population. "War is cruelty," he told Atlantans not long before their city went up in flames, "and you cannot refine it."

Sherman succeeded Grant as commander-in-chief of the army in 1869. His tenure in office saw completion of the transcontinental railroad and the waging of merciless war on the Plains Indian tribes. His excellent *Memoirs* appeared in 1875. He resisted all enticements to enter politics, for which he had a profound contempt. Sherman's off-the-cuff definition of war to an Ohio veterans' group in 1881 could stand as his epitaph: "It is all hell, boys." He died of pneumonia in New York City.

GEORGE H. THOMAS

1816–70
Birthplace:
Southhampton County,
Virginia
Senior Command:
Army of the Cumberland,
1863

A native of Virginia, George H. Thomas graduated from West Point in 1840 with W.T. Sherman and R.S. Ewell. Commissioned into the artillery, he participated in punitive campaigns against Native American tribes in Florida and on the Plains. His conduct during the Mexican War earned him brevets for gallantry at Monterrey and Buena Vista.

Despite being Southern-born, Thomas remained loyal to the Union. During the opening weeks of the war, he commanded a brigade in the Shenandoah Valley, after which he was sent to Kentucky to organize new recruits. In January 1862, Thomas served as second in command of the 1st Division Army of the Ohio, helping to secure a victory at Mill Springs. Later that spring, he commanded a division at Shiloh and in the advance on Corinth, Mississippi.

Later that year Thomas returned to Kentucky, where he turned down an offer to replace Don Carlos Buell as Army of the Ohio commander. When Rosecrans accepted the position, Thomas became commander of the XIV Corps, Army of the Cumberland, demonstrating his capability at Stone's River and during the 1863 Tullahoma Campaign.

Affectionately referred to by his troops as "Pap," his stout defense at Chickamauga in September 1863 earned him the sobriquet of the "Rock of Chickamauga," making him a national hero. His steady resolve during that battle allowed Rosecrans and his troops to retreat safely.

Having proved a reliable and capable leader, Thomas was promoted to command the Army of the Cumberland. On November 25, 1863, his troops launched an aggressive assault on Missionary Ridge that ended in a decisive Confederate defeat. He checked the advancing Army of Tennessee, led by John B. Hood, at Franklin, Tennessee, on November 30, 1864, after which he retreated to Nashville.

Despite Grant's repeated orders to launch an immediate offensive against Hood's forces, Thomas delayed, fearing that his army was too weak. Grant ordered a replacement to relieve Thomas of command, but Thomas's army rallied before the replacement arrived. On December 15, 1864, Thomas launched a crushing attack against the Confederates. Under his command, the Union army routed and nearly destroyed Hood's army, effectively ending Hood's career in the field. The Battle of Nashville was an overwhelming victory for the Union and one of the decisive battles of the war. Thomas was promoted to major general in the regular army and awarded the Thanks of Congress for his leadership.

THE
CONFEDERACY

Jefferson Davis,
President of the Confederacy

Pierre G.T. Beauregard

1818–93
Birthplace:
St. Bernard Parish, Louisiana
Senior Command:
Western Department, 1862

Born into a prosperous Louisiana Creole family, Pierre G.T. Beauregard graduated second in his class from West Point in 1838. He was commissioned into the engineer corps of the Old Army, where he worked on various fortifications in New Orleans. During the Mexican War, he served as an engineer on General Winfield Scott's staff, after which he returned to New Orleans.

After a brief five-day period as a superintendent at West Point, Beauregard was recalled due to his outspoken secessionist sympathies. On February 20, 1861, he resigned his U.S. commission and accepted a senior command as brigadier general in the Confederate army. He assumed command of the defenses at Charleston, South Carolina.

Beauregard directed Confederate forces in the bombardment of Fort Sumter, the incident that touched off the Civil War, on April 12, 1861. His success at Fort Sumter made him the Confederacy's first hero, and he became Joseph E. Johnston's second-in-command in northern

Virginia. On June 1, Beauregard assumed command of the army at Manassas. He was credited with the South's first significant victory, at Bull Run (Manassas) on July 21, 1861, and was soon promoted to full general.

Never a favorite of President Davis, Beauregard was bounced from one command to another. Second-in-command to A.S. Johnston at Shiloh in Tennessee, he took charge when Johnston was mortally wounded and wired a victory message to Richmond at the close of the first day's fighting. The wire proved a great embarrassment, for Grant reversed the Union's fortunes on the second day, driving Beauregard into retreat.

Beauregard's skillful defense of the communications center of Petersburg in June 1864 allowed Lee time to send reinforcements to check the Union offensive. The city held out for another ten months, until April 1865. Beauregard ended the war as Gen. J.E. Johnston's second-in-command in North Carolina.

Toward the war's end, Beauregard served as second-in-command to Joseph E. Johnston in the Carolinas. He surrendered with Johnston's army in April 1865.

Offered positions of senior command in the Rumanian and Egyptian armies after the war, Beauregard chose instead to head the New Orleans, Jackson, and Mississippi Railway, after which he managed the Louisiana lottery. In 1888 he was named commissioner of public works in New Orleans. Beauregard's extensive writings on the Civil War include *Report on the Defense of Charleston* (1864).

BRAXTON BRAGG

1817–76
Birthplace:
Warrenton, North Carolina
Senior Command:
Calvary Corps
Army of Tennessee, 1862–63

North Carolina-born Braxton Bragg, an 1837 West Pointer, showed leadership promise in his early career, especially as a capable organizer and artillerist. However, he inspired indifference in his troops and contempt, even hatred, in many of his fellow officers.

In 1861 Bragg was appointed brigadier general. Shortly after his participation in the April 1862 Battle of Shiloh, he was promoted to full general. Later that year his invasion of Kentucky ended in failure and retreat after the drawn battles of Perryville in October and Stone's River at year's end. His Army of Tennessee defeated Union forces at Chickamauga in September 1863, but Bragg failed to follow up this success. On November 23, Grant routed his demoralized army at Missionary Ridge, and a defeated Bragg retreated into Georgia. On December 2, 1863, Joseph E. Johnston assumed command of the Army of Tennessee.

Bragg served as President Davis's military adviser in 1864. Returning to the field in March 1865, he fought his last battle against Sherman in North Carolina.

NATHAN BEDFORD FORREST

1821–77
Birthplace:
Chapel Hill, Tennessee
Senior Command:
Cavalry Corps
Army of Tennessee, 1864–65

An indifferently educated blacksmith's son, Nathan Bedford Forrest built a fortune as a cotton planter and slave trader in his native Tennessee. When the Civil War broke out in 1861, Forrest enlisted as a private in a cavalry regiment he had raised and equipped at his own expense.

Within a few weeks, Forrest had risen to command the regiment as lieutenant colonel and embarked on the career that would make him the best-known and most feared Confederate cavalry commander of the Civil War. Despite his arguments against surrender of Fort Donelson in February 1862, his supervisor overruled him; he escaped, however, at the head of a detachment of cavalry. Two months later he was seriously wounded at the Battle of Shiloh.

When Forrest returned to the field during the summer of 1862, he led a series of destructive raids behind the Union lines, including one in Murfreesboro, Tennessee, where he captured 1,000 prisoners and supplies valued at $1,000,000, and destroyed key railroad lines. His skill as a commander enabled him to check Union cavalry penetrations of Confederate territory. Throughout 1864 he raided so successfully that William T. Sherman vowed to stop him "if it costs ten thousand lives and bankrupts the federal treasury."

In April 1864, Forrest's command carried out the infamous massacre of surrendering black troops at Fort Pillow, Tennessee. Despite his denial that he had ordered the killing of the several dozen black soldiers, it seems probable that Forrest was responsible, as he had repeatedly issued similar threats to Union soldiers.

Forrest continued to launch successful raids against the Union, severely depleting their supplies and capturing thousands of soldiers. During Hood's unsuccessful 1864 Tennessee campaign, Forrest commanded the Confederate cavalry. He was promoted to lieutenant general in February 1865, but the effectiveness of his troops began to erode. His command failed to check the Union Gen. James H. Wilson's raid to Selma, Alabama, in March and April 1865, the last great cavalry operation of the war. Overcome with hunger and exhaustion, Forrest was forced to surrender on May 4, 1865.

Two of Forrest's brothers were killed during the war, and his personal finances were seriously depleted. His brief presidency of a railroad resulted in bankruptcy. After the war, Forrest became involved with the Ku Klux Klan in his native state and is believed to have served as its Grand Wizard from 1867 until 1869.

Ambrose Powell Hill

1825–65
Birthplace:
Culpeper, Virginia.
Senior Command:
Corps Commander,
Army of Northern Virginia,
1863–65

A native of Virginia, A.P. Hill was a more effective commander than student. He needed five years to finish at West Point, although he finally graduated in 1847 in time to see front-line service in Mexico.

Hill resigned from the U.S. Army during the secession crisis and first achieved prominence as an infantry commander on the Virginia Peninsula in 1862, where he earned a reputation as one of the hardest-hitting of Lee's division commanders. Following the Battle of Williamsburg, he was promoted to major general. After Jackson was mortally wounded, Hill succeeded to corps command. As the lieutenant general of the newly created Third Corps, he fought at Gettysburg and in a number of heavy engagements during the Petersburg siege of 1864–65.

Hill once said that he had no wish to survive the collapse of the Confederacy. On April 2, 1865, during Grant's final successful assault on Petersburg, advancing Union troops shot him dead as he rode toward the front to rally his broken command.

THOMAS J. "STONEWALL" JACKSON

1824–63
Birthplace:
Clarksburg, Virginia
(now West Virginia)
Senior Command:
Corps Commander, Army of
Northern Virginia, 1862–63

Thomas J. "Stonewall" Jackson surmounted a poverty-blighted orphan childhood in Clarksburg, Virginia, to become the most brilliant and certainly the most famous of Robert E. Lee's lieutenants. He had little in the way of formal early schooling to prepare him for the military academy at West Point, and he arrived there in 1842 well behind his classmates. He worked hard, though, rising to 17th of 59 cadets in the class of 1846. Graduating with him were the future Civil War commanders George McClellan and A.P. Hill.

Jackson served with distinction in the Mexican War and saw action at Vera Cruz, Cerro Gordo, and Chapultepec, but he struggled in the peacetime army. Bored, restless, and quarrelsome, he resigned in 1852 to teach mathematics at the Virginia Military Institute in Lexington.

Like Ulysses S. Grant, Jackson showed little of the dash in civilian life that would mark his incomparable wartime career. Perhaps his formidable eccentricities stood in the way of success. His students called him "Tom Fool"

Jackson, and he seems to have been the very model of the absent-minded professor. His obsessive Presbyterian piety was legendary. Yet he lived a tranquil, satisfying domestic life. His first wife, Elinor Junkin, died in 1854. Three years later he married Mary Anna Morrison, who, like Elinor, was the daughter of a Presbyterian minister.

Jackson did not involve himself in the debate over secession, though he commanded the VMI cadet detachment at the hanging of the insurrectionary John Brown in 1859. He once described war as "the sum of all evils," but when the Civil War began in 1861, he promptly obtained a commission in the Confederate army.

He earned his famous *nom de guerre* early in the war. At a critical moment during the first battle of Bull Run, he repulsed a Federal assault with such aplomb that an officer commanding down the line sought to inspire his own troops by calling out: "Look! There is Jackson standing like a stone wall. Rally behind the Virginians!" His soldiers called him "Old Jack." Tall, thin, with a long trailing beard, he looked ordinary except for his eyes — they were pale blue and glittered brilliantly in battle, or so nearly everyone who knew him said. He neither smoked, drank, nor played cards, and sometimes refused to march or fight on Sundays. He wore a plain field uniform with few symbols of rank and had little patience with military pomp and ceremony.

A harsh disciplinarian, Jackson demanded a great deal of his men and of himself. "I never saw one of Jackson's couriers without expecting an order to assault the North Pole," recalled one officer who served under him. He fought with an intelligent slashing audacity that seemed to paralyze his opponents. "Always mystify, mislead, and surprise the enemy," he said. His Shenandoah Valley operation of 1862, which put those principles into practice, has been judged as near to perfect as any similar campaign in military history. Planned as a diversion to draw off troops from McClellan in the Virginia Peninsula, it served its purpose brilliantly.

At Kernstown on March 23, 1862, Jackson suffered a tactical reverse. He retreated slowly up the valley with superior Union forces under Nathaniel Banks close behind. Then Jackson struck, repulsing a Federal attack at McDowell on May 8. On May 23, he struck Banks at Front Royal, driving him back to Winchester. Renewing the attack on the 25th, he chased the Federals back across the Potomac. As a consequence, the Union high command, fearing Jackson would move next on Washington, suspended the march of an army corps bound for McClellan. This threw the Peninsula Campaign into disarray, and Jackson compounded the difficulty by closing out his valley operations with victories at Cross Keys and Port Republic on June 8 and 9.

Jackson's reputation slumped a bit after he joined Lee on the Peninsula for the Seven Days' battles. His chronic tardiness—he appears to have been suffering from strain and nervous exhaustion—may have cost Lee a decisive victory. However, he rebounded at the second battle of Bull Run, Antietam, and, most notably, Chancellorsville, where his flank march and assault on the Federal right wing set up Lee's masterpiece victory. Late in the afternoon of May 2, 1863, after a daylong tramp through dense woods, Jackson's 26,000 infantry approached the exposed flank of Oliver O. Howard's XI Corps.

Howard's command had stacked arms and called it a day when some of the men looked up to see deer, rabbits, and other wildlife bounding out of the thickets. Within moments, Confederate infantry burst out of the woods, shrieking the rebel yell. Jackson drove the Federals back two miles, almost to Chancellorsville itself. Not satisfied with a partial victory, he pushed to the front under a full moon to organize a night attack. A group of North Carolina soldiers mistook his mounted entourage for enemy cavalry and opened fire. Later that night, an army surgeon amputated Jackson's left arm just below the shoulder.

At first it looked as though he would recover. Then the dreaded complication of pneumonia set in. On Sunday, May 10, Jackson slipped into a delirium of fever, shouting out commands—"Pass the infantry to the front!"—and urging his aides to move faster, faster. He calmed down later in the day. "Let us cross over the river, and rest under the shade of the trees," he said finally, and then he died.

Lee offered a simple epitaph: "I know not how to replace him."

ALBERT SIDNEY JOHNSTON

1803–62
Birthplace:
Washington, Kentucky
Senior Command:
Army of Mississippi, 1862

A Kentucky-born Texan and an 1826 West Point graduate, Albert Sidney Johnston fought in the Black Hawk War, the Mexican War, and led U.S. troops in the Utah Expedition against the Mormons in 1858. When Texas seceded early in 1861, he declined an offer to serve as Winfield Scott's second-in-command, joining the Confederacy instead as its second-ranking general.

In 1861 President Davis judged him the most capable of his contemporaries, describing him as "the greatest soldier…living." His success at Bowling Green seemed to validate Davis's assessment, but the record of unbroken defeat that Johnston built in Kentucky and Tennessee in 1862, retreating from Fort Donelson through Nashville to northern Mississippi, quickly reversed it.

In April 1862, he led the Army of Mississippi on the first day of fighting at Shiloh, attacking Grant's Union army near the country church. During the assault he sustained a leg wound and bled to death on the battlefield.

JOSEPH E. JOHNSTON

1807–91
Birthplace:
Farmville, Virginia.
Senior Command:
Army of Tennessee, 1863–64

An 1829 West Point classmate of Robert E. Lee, Virginia-born Joseph E. Johnston ranks as one of the most skillful Southern commanders. With Beauregard, he led Confederate forces to a resounding victory at First Bull Run (Manassas). In sole command on the Virginia Peninsula, Johnston dropped back steadily before McClellan's forces. Wounded near Richmond, he yielded command to Lee and never returned to the eastern army.

In command of the Army of Tennessee in 1864, Johnston retreated toward Atlanta before Sherman's superior force. President Davis relieved him on July 17, charging that he had failed to bring Sherman to battle. He was replaced with John Bell Hood, whose impulsive and ill-advised offensives proved disastrous for the Army of Tennessee. Johnston returned to the field in February 1865 and surrendered to Sherman on April 26th.

Johnston's partisans claimed, rightly, that he never lost a decisive battle. On the other hand, this cautious commander never actually won one on his own, either.

ROBERT E. LEE

1807–70
Birthplace:
Alexandria, Virginia
Senior Command:
Army of Northern Virginia,
1862–65

One of history's greatest commanders, Robert E. Lee led the Army of Northern Virginia from July 1, 1862, to the Confederacy's end at Appomattox Courthouse on April 9, 1865. For nearly three years, the brilliant, daring, and resourceful Virginian fought the always larger, more powerful Union Army of the Potomac to a draw.

Born into Virginia's aristocracy, he was the son of the improvident Revolutionary War hero "Light Horse Harry" Lee, whose irresponsible financial dealings nearly ruined the family. When the elder Lee died, care of the invalid widow fell to young Robert. The boy shouldered the responsibility and continued to excel at his studies. He accepted the offer of a place at West Point—a free education and guaranteed employment upon graduation—in 1825, and made a brilliant record in his four years there, graduating second in his 1829 class of forty-six cadets.

In seventeen years in the prewar army, he saw varied service at outposts around the country. Lee fought in Mexico in 1846 to 1847 and was wounded there. He was superintendent of West Point from 1852 to 1855. In 1859 he commanded the detachment that captured the insurrectionary John Brown at Harpers Ferry, Virginia. On the outbreak of the Civil War, his superiors graded him the outstanding officer in U.S. service.

President Lincoln offered Lee command of Union forces after the attack on Fort Sumter. Though Lee opposed secession, Virginia's decision to leave the Union forced him to choose between his officer's oath and loyalty to his state. "I cannot raise my hand against my birthplace, my home, my children," he wrote a friend. In May 1861, he accepted a brigadier general's commission in the Confederate Army. His career as a commander started slowly. His first field campaign, in western Virginia later in 1861, ended in failure. After a brief service as President Jefferson Davis's military advisor, he assumed command of the Army of Northern Virginia in June 1862.

The Lee legend began to take shape almost at once, for he proved to be a commander of barely restrained boldness and audacity. The chances of battle stirred him to his depths. "It is well that war is so terrible," he once said, "or we should grow too fond of it."

With Union forces in sight of Richmond, Lee launched the counteroffensive known as the battles of the Seven Days (June 25–July 1, 1862) that drove the Federals away from the capital. Lee followed the Seven Days with an overwhelming success at Second Bull Run in late August. In September his first invasion of the North, a daring operation with political and diplomatic, as well as military aims, came to grief in the drawn battle of Antietam. Victory at Fredericksburg in December 1862 restored Lee's aura of invincibility.

In May 1863, he conducted the brilliant battle of maneuver that yielded his greatest triumph, Chancellorsville. Responding to a Federal offensive, he boldly divided his army, attacked the larger enemy force in groups, and drove the Federals back to their positions beyond the Rappahannock. Lee's reputation reached its zenith after Chancellorsville. The army retained an almost absolute faith in him. "We looked forward to victory under him as confidently as to successive sunrises," one of his officers, the artillerist Edward Porter Alexander, observed.

Lee's second great gamble, the Pennsylvania campaign of June-July 1863, ended in a decisive repulse at Gettysburg. The battle opened by accident, with an unplanned clash near Gettysburg on July 1. Lee concentrated his forces—once again, he had divided his army—and, against the advice of some of his leading lieutenants, decided to attack Gen. George Meade's army in a strong defensive position south of the town.

The consequence was the largest, bloodiest battle ever fought in North America. The sound of the guns of Gettysburg could be heard as far as Pittsburgh 150 miles west. It ended with Pickett's disastrous charge up Cemetery Ridge on the afternoon of July 3. Lee himself met the tattered survivors of the charge. "It is all my fault," he said as he rode among them. "It is I who have lost this fight."

Lee withdrew the army into Virginia, and from then on the Confederates fought on the defensive. By mid–1864, the Federal commander, Ulysses S. Grant, had forced the once-nimble Army of Northern Virginia into static lines covering Richmond and Petersburg. "This army cannot stand a siege," Lee remarked to one of his officers, and in due course events bore him out. The army slowly disintegrated during the cold, hungry winter of 1864–1865. Grant's final campaign was short and decisive. By the morning of April 9, Union forces had trapped Lee's once-vaunted army near the village of Appomattox Court House. "There is nothing left for me to do but go and see General Grant," Lee told his staff, "and I would rather die a thousand deaths."

Even in his own day, Lee attained mythic stature. Handsome, courtly, unfailingly kind in manner, and legendary for his tenderness to animals, he inspired in his troops deep confidence and devotion. A religious man, he became for many the ideal of the Christian soldier. As a tactical commander, Lee knew no peer. Critics have faulted him, however, for a strategic short-sightedness that placed the defense of his beloved Virginia above all else.

The U.S. authorities left Lee alone after the war. He applied for a parole in July 1865, in part as an example to diehard Confederates. In the autumn of 1865 he accepted the presidency of Washington College (now Washington and Lee) in Lexington, Virginia. He died there of a heart ailment on October 12, 1870.

JAMES LONGSTREET

1821 – 1904
Birthplace:
Edgefield District,
South Carolina
Senior Command:
Corps Commander
Army of Northern Virginia,
1862 – 65

Lee's "Old War Horse," Longstreet was prosaic, reliable, brave as a lion. Born in South Carolina, raised in Georgia and Alabama, he graduated from West Point in 1842 near the bottom of his class, with such notable soldiers as Ulysses S. Grant and William T. Sherman.

Commissioned into the Old Army as an infantry second lieutenant, Longstreet fought with Zachary Taylor in the Mexican War and participated in the march on Mexico City with Winfield Scott. His actions at Churubusco and Molino del Rey earned him brevets to captain and major. He transferred into the paymaster corps, declaring that he had "abandoned all dreams of military glory," a statement he began to revise during the secession crisis.

Loyalty to the South inspired Longstreet to resign from the paymaster corps in 1861 and accept a Confederate commission as brigadier general. A veteran of First Bull Run (Manassas) and the Seven Days' battles, Longstreet found his true vocation as a corps commander under Lee—a methodical, precise, and hard-hitting complement to the elusive, fast-moving Jackson. His dogged reliability earned him promotion to lieutenant general late in 1862 and the charge of the newly organized First Corps.

Longstreet's corps launched the powerful counterattack that broke Pope's army at the Second Battle of Bull Run (Manassas) and bore the greater share of the fighting at Marye's Heights at Fredericksburg. Stubborn and self-assured, Longstreet did not hesitate to challenge Lee, especially after Jackson's death. He vigorously opposed the Pennsylvania campaign of 1863 and tried to argue Lee out of attacking at Gettysburg in July. Events, especially the debacle of Pickett's charge, proved him right.

Accidentally wounded by his own men in the Wilderness in the spring of 1864, Longstreet returned to duty in the autumn and served with the Army of Northern Virginia to the end, despite a paralyzed right arm. In the remaining months, he took part in the last battles, at Petersburg and Richmond. On April 9, 1865, Longstreet surrendered with Lee.

Although Longstreet was highly regarded by his own men, he became a deeply controversial postwar figure, not least because he embraced the Republican party. Moreover, "Lost Cause" diehards unfairly stigmatized him for the defeat at Gettysburg and its ultimate consequence, the collapse of the Confederacy. His memoir *From Manassas to Appomattox* (1896), in which he criticized Lee and Jackson, only increased his unpopularity with Southerners.

John C. Pemberton

1814–81
Birthplace:
Philadelphia, Pennsylvania
Senior Command:
Departments of Mississippi,
Tennessee, and East
Louisiana, 1862–63

Pennsylvania-born John Pemberton, an 1837 West Pointer, had a long and adventurous career in the Old Army, serving in Mexico, on the frontier, and with the Utah Expedition. Married into a Virginia family, he elected to fight for the Confederacy in 1861.

From an 1861 assignment to organize Virginia's artillery and cavalry, Pemberton was quickly and unwisely promoted beyond his abilities. In October 1862, he assumed command of the Departments of Mississippi, Tennessee, and East Louisiana. At Vicksburg in 1863 he proved himself no match for Grant. After a short campaign of tactical maneuver and a six-week siege, in which he was both outwitted and outnumbered, Pemberton surrendered the strategic Mississippi River fortress on July 4, 1863.

Southerners unfairly suspected the Northern-born Pemberton of treachery at Vicksburg. Taken captive and later exchanged, he served out the war in a backwater ordnance inspectorate in Virginia.

James Ewell Brown "Jeb" Stuart

1833–64
Birthplace:
Patrick County, Virginia
Senior Command:
Calvary Corps,
Army of Northern Virginia

The Stuarts were a well-to-do Virginia planter family. The seventh of ten children, "Jeb," as he was known from the initial letters of his names, grew up at Laurel Hill, the Stuart home place in Patrick County. His father, prominent locally, served a term in the U.S. Congress. Jeb was educated at home, and at Emory and Henry College. He entered West Point in 1850.

Stuart did well at the academy, though he was prone to fighting. Otherwise well-behaved, he was quietly religious and popular with most of his classmates. He graduated a solid 13th in the 1854 class of 46 cadets.

Stuart served in Texas and Kansas before the war. During the Kansas border troubles, he encountered the abolitionist John Brown. In 1859, serving as an unpaid aide to Robert E. Lee while on leave, he identified Brown as the leader of the raid on the Harpers Ferry government arsenal that Lee's command quelled. As early as January 1861, he applied to Confederate president Jefferson Davis for a commission in the Southern army.

As colonel of the 1st Virginia Cavalry, Stuart led a well-timed charge at the first battle of Bull Run (Manassas) that contributed to the Confederate victory on that field. Within a few weeks, he received promotion to command of a cavalry brigade. During the spring of 1862, the brigade performed excellent service screening the army during the withdrawal up the Virginia Peninsula.

On June 11, with orders to reconnoiter Federal positions, Stuart set out with 1,200 troopers on the first of his famous rides around the Army of the Potomac. Having thoroughly embarrassed the Union forces, he returned four days later with 165 prisoners and 260 captured horses and mules.

The raid won Stuart promotion to major general and command of all the Army of Northern Virginia's cavalry. Rising swiftly to prominence as leader of the "eyes and ears" of Lee's army, he continued his raiding career during the second Bull Run campaign with a visit to the Union Gen. John Pope's headquarters, where he made off with important documents and one of Pope's uniforms. In October, a second ride around the Union army took him to Chambersburg, Pennsylvania. This 126-mile gallop with 1,800 men—the final 80 miles without a halt—solidified Stuart's reputation for brilliance and dash, and netted the Confederacy another 500 captured horses.

Stuart was a striking, even elegant, figure, solidly built, with a flowing red beard. He wore a handsome gray cape trimmed in red and a cavalier's cocked hat with a gilt star and a long peacock's plume. He rode a powerful charger.

At numerous parties and balls, he cut a fine figure as a dancer. But Stuart led a quietly conventional and sober private life, in spite of his romantic appearance and buccaneering military ways.

His detractors accused him of glory hunting, but Stuart carried out a cavalry commander's routine tasks faithfully. In December 1862, during the Fredericksburg campaign, he launched several strikes against Union communications. His Dumfries Raid at year's end cost the enemy heavily in stolen horses and burned supplies. Stuart kept Lee fully informed of Union movements during the initial phases of the Chancellorsville campaign in late April 1863. When Jackson was wounded on the night of May 2, he handled the II Corps infantry with competence in the final stages of the battle.

As time went on, Stuart found his Federal adversary much improved. His command recovered from an early morning surprise to fight a drawn battle with Union cavalry at Brandy Station in June, the largest mounted engagement of the war. The Confederates inflicted 1,000 casualties on the enemy troopers, double their own losses. After Brandy Station, Stuart effectively screened Lee's flank on the northward march toward Gettysburg, fighting off probing Federal cavalry in skirmishes at Aldie, Middleburg and Upperville in mid-June.

Only his failure to inform Lee of Union movements during the later stages of the Gettysburg campaign in June 1863 marred an otherwise exemplary war record. He set out on June 24 on another of his long jaunts around the enemy—and nearly ruined his military reputation this time. He harassed Union communications in Maryland and Pennsylvania, fought several skirmishes and carried off 125 wagons and 400 prisoners. Lee had little use for wagons and less for prisoners, however. What he wanted was word of his adversary's whereabouts. But Stuart had allowed the Army of the Potomac to get between his cavalry and Lee's main columns. Thus he hovered over the horizon and out of touch for several days, depriving Lee of critical intelligence in the period leading up to the battle of Gettysburg. Lee upbraided him severely—the only time in their association the commanding general had ever shown displeasure with Stuart's work.

Stuart's cavalry covered Lee's movements during the opening phases of the Wilderness and Spotsylvania campaigns of May 1864. On May 9, he led out with 4,500 troopers in pursuit of Union Gen. Philip Sheridan's 12,000-strong Cavalry Corps. Stuart reached Yellow Tavern outside Richmond just ahead of Sheridan early on May 11 and took up a position astride the main road to the capital. In an all-day fight, Stuart turned Sheridan away from Richmond, but the success cost him his life. Shot in the abdomen late in the afternoon, he died in Richmond the next day.

Stuart's plumed hats, theatrical capes and flowing beard were legendary in the Confederacy. Lee looked past his appearance to assess his military worth in one pithy line: "He never brought me a false piece of information."

EARL VAN DORN

1820–63
Birthplace:
Port Gibson, Mississippi
Senior Command:
Trans-Mississippi
Department,
Army of the West

Trained at West Point, from which he graduated in 1842, Earl Van Dorn fought in Mexico and on the frontier. Assigned to senior command in the Confederate army, he assumed control of the Confederate Trans-Mississippi Department early in 1862.

In March 1862, Union forces, under the leadership of Samuel Curtis, defeated Van Dorn and his Army of the West at Pea Ridge, Arkansas. In October, the Army of the West Tennessee, under his command, was routed at Corinth, and forced to retreat into central Mississippi. Although he was absolved of any responsibility for the Corinth defeat, Van Dorn was transferred to the cavalry as an independent commander. He returned to the field on December 20, when he led Pemberton's cavalry in a successful offensive at Holly Springs, Mississippi, where he captured the Union's supply base.

Van Dorn was fatally shot in a lover's quarrel in May 1863. The assailant claimed that his victim had been carrying on an affair with his wife.

INDEX